TWILIGHT TIME

TWILIGHT TIME

Quiet Thoughts to Sample and Savor at Bedtime

Selected by Peter Seymour

The C. R. Gibson Company
Norwalk, Connecticut

Introduction

The Day is done, and the darkness
Falls from the wings of Night,
As a feather is wafted downward
From an eagle in his flight.

S o begins Longfellow's poem "The Day Is Done" with
feelings of calm and quiet, a kind of softness in the air
descending and encircling us with a sense of peace and
serenity.

And so this book is intended to give you the same feelings,
as you take a few minutes or perhaps half an hour before bed
to browse its pages. The eagle—the swift day full of power and
motion—is gone. And now is a quiet time—moments for
reflection, meditation or just a little while to visit with passages
of prose and verse that offer insight, inspiration, cheer, comfort,
gentle humor or simply beautiful thoughts.

We all experience how different days bring different
problems, challenges, incidents. We approach bedtime,
therefore, in different moods—sometimes content, other times
confused, unhappy, restless, anticipating tomorrow with joy or
distaste. This book contains writings that can help mellow a
variety of such moods—"words to relax by," you might call
them; brief passages, poems, lovely descriptions, prayers, little
stories, inspiring pieces and friendly advice to sample and savor
just before the Sandman arrives.

Many of the world's great writers are included in this
book—traditional and modern, but always speaking with
modulated voices. There's no adventure here, no conflicts, high
drama, passions, great excitements! No—the selections have
been chosen for their warmth, compassion, tranquility . . . the
sort of placid, restful pleasures to build sweet dreams upon.

DREAM-SONG

Sunlight, moonlight,
Twilight, starlight—
Gloaming at the close of day,
And an owl calling,
Cool dews falling
In a wood of oak and may.

Lantern-light, taper-light,
Torchlight, no-light:
Darkness at the shut of day,
And lions roaring,
Their wrath pouring
In wild waste places far away.

Elf-light, bat-light,
Touchwood-light and toad-light,
And the sea a shimmering gloom of grey,
And a small face smiling
In a dream's beguiling
In a world of wonders far away.

WALTER DE LA MARE

WATCHING THE LITTLE WONDERS

This is the fullness of late summer now; the green of what is growing and grown conceals. I can watch a muskrat feed on a bank for ten minutes, harvesting shocks of grass that bristle and droop from his jaws, and when he is gone I cannot see any difference in the grass. If I spread the patch with my hands and peer closely, I am hard put to locate any damage from even the most intense grazing. Nothing even looks trampled. Does everything else but me pass so lightly? When the praying mantis egg cases hatched in June, over a period of several days, I watched the tiny translucent mantises leap about leggily on the egg case, scraggle down the hedge's twigs, and disappear in the grass. In some places I could see them descend in a line like a moving bridge from stem to ground. The instant they crossed the horizon and entered the grass, they vanished as if they had jumped off the edge of the world.

Now it is early September, and the paths are clogged. I look to water to see sky. It is the time of year when a honeybee beats feebly at the inside back window of every parked car. A frog flies up for every foot of bank, bubbles tangle in a snare of blue-green algae, and Japanese beetles hunch doubled on the willow leaves. The sun thickens the air to jelly; it bleaches, flattens, dissolves. The skies are a milky haze—nowhere, do-nothing summer skies. Every kid I see has a circular grid on his forehead, a regular cross-hatching of straight lines, from spending his days leaning into screen doors.

ANNIE DILLARD

OPTIMISM

Talk happiness. The world is sad enough
Without your woes. No path is wholly rough;
Look for the places that are smooth and clear,
And speak of those, to rest the weary ear
Of Earth, so hurt by one continuous strain
Of human discontent and grief and pain.

Talk faith. The world is better off without
Your uttered ignorance and morbid doubt.
If you have faith in God, or man, or self,
Say so. If not, push back upon the shelf
Of silence all your thoughts, till faith shall come;
No one will grieve because your lips are dumb.

Talk health. The dreary, never-changing tale
Of mortal maladies is worn and stale.
You cannot charm, or interest, or please
By harping on that minor chord, disease.
Say you are well, or all is well with you,
And God shall hear your words and make them true.

ELLA WHEELER WILCOX

JOY

Joy is the delightful experience of the feelings of pleasure at a good gained and actually enjoyed or the prospect of good which one has a reasonable hope of obtaining. There can be both natural joys and spiritual joys. Natural joys would be the joy of youth before disappointment has stretched the soul, or the joy of health when food is pleasant and sweet, or the joy of success when the battle has been won, or the joys of affection when the heart is loved. All these natural joys are intensified by spiritual joys and put upon a more enduring basis. No earthly happiness would be permanent or thorough if it were not associated with a good conscience.

Spiritual joy is a serenity of temper in the midst of the changes of life, such as a mountain has when a storm breaks over it. To a man who has never rooted the soul in the Divine every trouble exaggerates itself. He cannot put his full powers to any one thing because he is troubled about many things.

A joy is not the same as levity. Levity is an act, joy a habit. Mirth is like a meteor, cheerfulness like a star; mirth is like crackling thorns, joy like a fire. Joy being more permanent makes difficult actions easier. Soldiers after a long day's march would hardly walk as nimbly as they do, if they did not march to music. A cheerful heart always finds a yoke easy and a burden light.

Certainly no nurse is helpful in a sick room unless she has the spirit of cheerfulness. Every nurse really ought to have two things before she enters a sick room: an incision and a sense of humor. An incision in order that she may know the value of pain; a sense of humor in order that she may know how to diffuse happiness. This incision need not be physical but it should at least be symbolic, in the sense that there should be a deep appreciation of the woes and sufferings of others. There is nothing that so much adds to the longevity of sickness as a long face.

Joy has much more to do with the affections than with reason. To the man with a family his wife and children call out and sustain his delights much more than his intellect could ever stimulate. Standing before a cradle a father seems face to face with the attributes of the everlasting Being Who has infused His tenderness and love into the babe. The power of rejoicing is always a fair test of a man's moral condition. No man can be happy on the outside who is already unhappy on the inside. If a sense of guilt weighs down the soul no amount of pleasure on the outside can compensate for the loss of joy on the inside. As sorrow is attendant on sin, so joy is the companion of holiness.

Joy can be felt in both prosperity and adversity. In prosperity it consists not in the goods we enjoy but in those we hope for; not in the pleasures we experience but in the promise of those which we believe without our seeing. Riches may abound but those for which we hope are the kind which moths do not eat, rust consume, nor thieves break through and steal. Even in adversity there can be joy in the assurance that the Divine Master Himself died through the Cross as the condition of His Resurrection.

If joy be uncommon today it is because there are timid souls who have not the courage to forget themselves and to make sacrifices for their neighbor, or else because the narrower sympathies make the brighter things of the world to come, appear as vanities. As the pull from the belief in God and the salvation of the soul fade from life, so also joy vanishes and one returns to the despair of the heathens. The old Greeks and Romans always saw a shadow across their path and a skeleton at their feet. It was no surprise that one day a Roman who had nothing to live for, nothing to hope for, entered his bath and opened a vein and so bled quietly and painlessly to death. A famous Greek poet once said of life that it was better not to be born, and the next best thing was to quit life as soon as possible. All this is at the other extreme from St. Paul, who said: "Rejoice in the Lord always and again I say, Rejoice."

FULTON J. SHEEN

IDEALISM

Grown-up people reconcile themselves too willingly to a supposed duty of preparing young ones for the time when they will regard as illusion what now is an inspiration to heart and mind. Deeper experience of life, however, advises their inexperience differently. It exhorts them to hold fast, their whole life through, to the thoughts which inspire them. It is through the idealism of youth that man catches sight of truth, and in that idealism he possesses a wealth which he must never exchange for anything else. We must all be prepared to find that life tries to take from us our belief in the good and the true, and our enthusiasm for them, but we need not surrender them. That ideals, when they are brought into contact with reality, are usually crushed by facts does not mean that they are bound from the very beginning to capitulate to the facts, but merely that our ideals are not strong enough; and they are not strong enough because they are not pure and strong and stable enough in ourselves.

The power of ideals is incalculable. We see no power in a drop of water. But let it get into a crack in the rock and be turned to ice, and it splits the rock; turned into steam, it drives the pistons of the most powerful engines. Something has happened to it which makes active and effective the power that is latent in it.

ALBERT SCHWEITZER

FLYING ALONE

In the following selection, Charles Lindbergh describes his feelings immediately after take-off on his historic flight from New York to Paris.

I'm alone at last, over the first short stretch of sea on the route to France. The surface is calm. There's hardly a sign of movement beneath the oil-smooth sheen of its skin. It's only 35 miles to the Connecticut shore, but I've never flown across that much water before. The Sound comes as an advance messenger, welcoming and at the same time warning me of the empire that lies ahead—of the trackless wastes, the great solitude, the desertlike beauty of the ocean.

Haze thickens behind me until the coast line becomes lost. There's not a boat in sight. Only a few spiraling gulls and dark bits of refuse on the water show that land is near. I'm the center point in a circle of haze moving along with me over the glassy water—gray haze over gray water, the one mirrored in the other until I can't tell where sea ends and sky begins.

I relax in my cockpit—this little box with fabric walls, in which I'm to ride across the ocean. Now, if all goes well, I won't move from it for a day and a half, until I step out on French sod at the airport of Le Bourget. It's a compact place to live, designed to fit around me so snugly that no ounce of weight or resistance is wasted. I can press both sides of the fuselage with partly outstretched elbows. The instrument board is an easy reach forward for my hand, and a thin rib on the

roof is hollowed slightly to leave clearance for my helmet. There's room enough, no more, no less; my cockpit has been tailored to me like a suit of clothes.

A pilot doesn't feel at home in a plane until he's flown it for thousands of miles. At first it's like moving into a new house. The key doesn't slip in the door smoothly; the knobs and light switches aren't where you put your hand; the stairs don't have proper spacing, and the windows bind as you raise them. Later, after you've used the key a hundred times, it fits at once, turns easily in the lock. Knobs and switches leap to meet your fingers on the darkest night. The steps touch your feet in perfect timing; and windows slide open with an easy push. My test flights in California, the long hours of night above deserts and mountains of the Southwest, the swift trip over the Alleghenies to New York, have removed the feel of newness from the *Spirit of St. Louis.* Each dial and lever is in proper place for glance or touch; and the slightest pressure on controls brings response. My ears have become accustomed to the radial engine's tempo. It blends with the instrument readings and the clearing mist to instill a feeling of confidence and hope.

I'm glad this flight to Paris hasn't become a race. Now I can set my throttle for range instead of speed, hoarding gallons of gasoline for that worried hour when extra fuel means the saving of a flight. I never wanted to race across the ocean. There are hazards enough without adding human competition.

What advantages there are in flying alone! I know now what my father meant when he warned me, years ago, of depending too heavily on others. He used to quote a saying of old settlers in Minnesota: "One boy's a boy. Two boys are half a boy. Three boys are no boy at all." That had to do with hunting, trapping, and scouting in days when Indians were hostile. But how well it applies to modern life, and to this flight I'm making. By flying alone I've gained in range, in time, in flexibility; and above all, I've gained in freedom. I haven't had to keep a crew member acquainted with my plans. My movements weren't restricted by someone else's temperament, health, or knowledge. My decisions aren't weighted by responsibility for another's life. When I learned last night that the weather was improving, I had no one to consult; I needed only to order the *Spirit of St. Louis* readied for daybreak. When I was sitting in my cockpit, on the muddy runway, in the tail wind, there was no one to warp my judgment with a "Hell, let's try it!" or, "It looks pretty bad to me." I've not been enmeshed in petty quarreling and heavy organizational problems. Now, I can go on or turn back according to the unhampered dictates of my mind and senses. According to that saying of my father's, I'm a full boy—independent—alone.

THE FREEDOM OF THE MOON

I've tried the new moon tilted in the air
Above a hazy tree-and-farmhouse cluster
As you might try a jewel in your hair.
I've tried it fine with little breadth of luster,
Alone, or in one ornament combining
With one first-water star almost as shining.

I put it shining anywhere I please.
By walking slowly on some evening later,
I've pulled it from a crate of crooked trees
And brought it over glossy water, greater,
And dropped it in, and seen the image wallow,
The color run, all sorts of wonder follow.

ROBERT FROST

TONIGHT

For all who watch tonight—by land or sea or air—
O Father, may they know that Thou art with them there.

For all who weep tonight, the hearts that cannot rest,
Reveal Thy love, that wondrous love which gave for us Thy
     best.

For all who wake tonight, love's tender watch to keep,
Watcher Divine, Thyself draw nigh, Thou who dost never
     sleep.

For all who fear tonight, whate'er the dread may be,
We ask for them the perfect peace of hearts that rest in Thee.

Our own belov'd tonight, O Father, keep, and where
Our love and succor cannot reach, now bless them through our
     prayer.

And all who pray tonight, Thy wrestling hosts, O Lord,
Make weakness strong, let them prevail according to Thy word.

AUTHOR UNKNOWN

PLEASURE

In life there is nothing more unexpected and surprising than the arrivals and departures of pleasure. If we find it in one place today, it is vain to seek it there tomorrow. You cannot lay a trap for it. It will fall into no ambuscade, concert it ever so cunningly. Pleasure has no logic; it never treads in its own footsteps. Into our commonplace existence it comes with a surprise, like a pure white swan from the airy void into the ordinary village lake; and just as the swan, for no reason that can be discovered, lifts itself on its wings and betakes itself to the void again, *it* leaves us, and our sole possession is its memory. And it is characteristic of pleasure that we can never recognize it to be pleasure till after it is gone. Happiness never lays its finger on its pulse. If we attempt to steal a glimpse of its features it disappears. It is a gleam of unreckoned gold. From the nature of the case, our happiness, such as in its degree it has been, lives in memory. We have not the voice itself; we have only its echo. We are never happy; we can only remember that we were so once. And while in the very heart and structure of the happy moment there lurked an obscure consciousness of death, the memory in which past happiness dwells is always a regretful memory. This is why the tritest utterance about the past, youth, early love, and the like, has always about it an indefinable flavour of poetry, which pleases and affects. In the wake of a ship there is always a melancholy splendour. The finest set of verses of our modern time described how the poet gazed on the "happy autumn fields," and remembered the "days that were no more." After all, man's real possession is his memory. In nothing else is he rich, in nothing else is he poor.

ALEXANDER SMITH

MIRACLES

From E. B. White's beautiful story Charlotte's Web *we learn a little about miracles. Charlotte, of course, is the spider who has spun a web that says "Terrific" in praise of a pig named Wilbur. Mrs. Arable, who is distressed about her eight-year-old daughter Fern's involvement in all of this, has a chat with Dr. Dorian.*

"I've been hearing things about that pig," said Dr. Dorian, opening his eyes. "They say he's quite a pig."

"Have you heard about the words that appeared in the spider's web?" asked Mrs. Arable nervously.

"Yes," replied the doctor.

"Well, do you understand it?" asked Mrs. Arable.

"Understand what?"

"Do you understand how there could be any writing in a spider's web?"

"Oh, no," said Dr. Dorian. "I don't understand it. But for that matter I don't understand how a spider learned to spin a web in the first place. When the words appeared, everyone said they were a miracle. But nobody pointed out that the web itself is a miracle."

"What's miraculous about a spider's web?" said Mrs. Arable. "I don't see why you say a web is a miracle—it's just a web."

"Ever try to spin one?" asked Dr. Dorian.

Mrs. Arable shifted uneasily in her chair. "No," she replied. "But I can crochet a doily and I can knit a sock."

"Sure," said the doctor. "But somebody taught you, didn't they?"

"My mother taught me."

"Well, who taught a spider? A young spider knows how to

spin a web without any instructions from anybody. Don't you regard that as a miracle?"

"I suppose so," said Mrs. Arable. "I never looked at it that way before. Still, I don't understand how those words got into the web. I don't understand it, and I don't like what I can't understand."

"None of us do," said Dr. Dorian, sighing. "I'm a doctor. Doctors are supposed to understand everything. But I don't understand everything, and I don't intend to let it worry me."

Mrs. Arable fidgeted. "Fern says the animals talk to each other. Dr. Dorian, do you believe animals talk?"

"I never heard one say anything," he replied. "But that proves nothing. It is quite possible that an animal has spoken civilly to me and that I didn't catch the remark because I wasn't paying attention. Children pay better attention than grownups. If Fern says that the animals in Zuckerman's barn talk, I'm quite ready to believe her. Perhaps if people talked less, animals would talk more. People are incessant talkers—I can give you my word on that."

THE STARS

Battling my way homeward one dark night against the wind and rain, a sudden gust, stronger than the others, drove me back into the shelter of a tree. But soon the Western sky broke open; the illumination of the Stars poured down from behind the dispersing clouds.

I was astonished at their brightness, to see how they filled the night with their lustre. So I went my way accompanied by them; Arcturus followed me, and becoming entangled in a leafy tree, shone by glimpses, and then emerged triumphant, Lord of the Western sky. Moving along the road in my waterproof and galoshes, my thoughts were among the Constellations. I too was one of the Princes of the starry Universe; in me also there was something that blazed, that glittered.

LOGAN PEARSALL SMITH

FLOWER IN THE CRANNIED WALL

Flower in the crannied wall,
I pluck you out of the crannies,
I hold you here, root and all, in my hand,
Little flower—but *if* I could understand
What you are, root and all, and all in all,
I should know what God and man is.

ALFRED, LORD TENNYSON

LITTLE THINGS

There's nothing very beautiful and nothing very gay
About the rush of faces in the town by day;
But a light tan cow in a pale green mead,
That is very beautiful, beautiful indeed.
And the soft March wind, and the low March mist
Are better than kisses in a dark street kissed.
The fragrance of the forest when it wakes at dawn,
The fragrance of a trim green village lawn,
The hearing of the murmur of the rain at play—
These things are beautiful, beautiful as day!
And I shan't stand waiting for love or scorn
When the feast is laid for a day new-born . . .
Oh, better let the little things I loved when little
Return when the heart finds the great things brittle;
And better is a temple made of bark and thong
Than a tall stone temple that may stand too long.

ORRICK JOHNS

BEAUTY

Beauty means this to one person, perhaps, and that to the other. And yet when any one of us has seen or heard or read that which to him is beautiful, he has known an emotion which is in every case the same in kind, if not in degree; an emotion precious and uplifting. A choirboy's voice, a ship in sail, an opening flower, a town at night, the song of the blackbird, a lovely poem, leaf shadows, a child's grace, the starry skies, a cathedral, apple trees in spring, a thorough-bred horse, sheep-bells on a hill, a rippling stream, a butterfly, the crescent moon—the thousand sights or sounds or words that evoke in us the thought of beauty—these are the drops of rain that keep the human spirit from death by drought. They are a stealing and a silent refreshment that we perhaps do not think about but which goes on all the time. The war brought a kind of revolt against beauty in art, literature, and music, a revolt that is already passing, and that I am sure will pass. It would surprise any of us if we realized how much store we unconsciously set by beauty, and how little savour there would be left in life if it were withdrawn. It is the smile on the earth's face, open to all, and needs but the eyes to see, the mood to understand.

JOHN GALSWORTHY

AMERICAN FLAG PLANTED

The two men walked easily, talked easily, even ran and jumped happily so it seemed. They picked up rocks, talked at length of what they saw, planted an American flag, saluted it, and talked by radiophone with the President in the White House, and then faced the camera and saluted Mr. Nixon.

"For every American, this has to be the proudest day of our lives," the President told the astronauts. "For one priceless moment in the whole history of man, all the people on this earth are truly one."

Seven hours earlier, at 4:17 P.M., the Eagle and its two pilots thrilled the world as they zoomed in over a rock-covered field, hovered and then slowly let down on the moon. "Houston, Tranquillity base here," Armstrong radioed. "The Eagle has landed."

At 1:10 A.M. Monday—2 hours and 14 minutes after Armstrong first stepped upon the lunar surface—the astronauts were back in their moon craft and the hatch was closed.

In describing the moon, Armstrong told Houston that it was "fine and powdery. I can kick it up loosely with my toe.

"It adheres like powdered charcoal to the boot," he went on, "but I only go in a small fraction of an inch. I can see my footprint in the moon like fine grainy particles."

Armstrong found he had such little trouble walking on the moon that he began talking almost as if he didn't want to leave it.

"It has a stark beauty all its own," Armstrong said. "It's like the desert in the Southwestern United States. It's very pretty out here."

THOMAS O'TOOLE

RIVER MOONS

The double moon, one on the high backdrop of the west, one
     on the curve of the river face,
The sky moon of fire and the river moon of water, I am taking
     these home in a basket, hung on an elbow, such a teeny
     weeny elbow, in my head.
I saw them last night, a cradle moon, two horns of a moon,
     such an early hopeful moon, such a child's moon for all
     young hearts to make a picture of.
The river—I remember this like a picture—the river was the
     upper twist of a written question mark.
I know now it takes many many years to write a river, a
     twist of water asking a question.
And white stars moved when the moon moved, and one red star
     kept burning, and the Big Dipper was almost overhead.

CARL SANDBURG

UPS AND DOWNS, INS AND OUTS

I have asked hundreds of audiences around the world
For a show of hands by those
Who do not use the words "up" and "down."
In none of all my audiences have hands appeared.
This means that all the human beings
In all of my audiences
Use the words "up" and "down,"
And believe they're being logical
In so doing.
And they query,
"What may we say cogently
In lieu of *up* and *down?*"
The answer was found by aviators.
As they flew around the world.
They did not feel themselves
To be "upside down."
As flyers they selected the right words.
Flyers "Come *in* for a landing."
Flyers "Go *out* in the sky."
Flyers "Fly *around* the world."
And the astronauts
Go *in* toward various celestial bodies
And accelerate *out*wardly from them
And *into* the spatial nothingness
Out of which space they steer themselves
To come *in* to another
Of the always orbiting celestial bodies,
Around any of which they may locally orbit
In great or lesser circles.

All of us go *out*ward, *in*ward and *around*
Any object, or system of reference,
Such as planets, stars, houses, things, and atoms.
Atomic events transpire
*In*ward, *out*ward and *around* their respective nuclei.
We direct an astronaut *into* the Moon:
We will soon direct him *into* Mars.
Out is common to all bodies
And is *out*ward in all directions
From any one of them.

"Out" is omnidirectional,
"In" is unidirectional.
"In" is unique.
In is always specifically oriented.
In is *in*dividual.

The word "invention"
Uses the prefix "in"
To identify this specifically.
It means a "coming in,"
A coming into our thought of a unique conception,
Which we *in* turn
Realize *in* a special physical case demonstration
Thus in-troducing
The in-vention to society.

No scientist would suggest that any part of the Universe
Is identifiable as "up"
Nor any other locale as "down."
Yet individual scientists themselves
As yet reflex spontaneously
In an "up" and "down," conditioned-reflex miasma.

Their senses say reflexively,
"I see the Sun is going down,"
Despite that scientists
And almost everyone else have known theoretically
For five hundred years that the Sun is not going down at dusk
And rising at dawn.
What is important in this connection
Is that the way in which humans reflex spontaneously
For that is the way in which
They usually behave in critical moments,
And it is often "common sense" to reflex
In perversely ignorant ways
That produce social disasters
By denying knowledge
And ignorantly yielding to common sense.

R. BUCKMINSTER FULLER

TAMING THE BICYCLE

At one point in his life, Mark Twain claims to have taken lessons on how to ride a bicycle. After much practice, with the help of various "instructors," Twain is at last ready to try a complete U-turn on the bike.

This is not a pleasant thing, when you undertake it for the first time on your own responsibility, and neither is it likely to succeed. Your confidence oozes away, you fill steadily up with nameless apprehensions, every fiber of you is tense with a watchful strain, you start a cautious and gradual curve, but your squirmy nerves are all full of electric anxieties, so the curve is quickly demoralized into a jerky and perilous zigzag; then suddenly the nickel-clad horse takes the bit in its mouth and goes slanting for the curbstone, defying all prayers and all your powers to change its mind—your heart stands still, your breath hangs fire, your legs forget to work, straight on you go, and there are but a couple of feet between you and the curb now. And now is the desperate moment, the last chance to save yourself; of course all your instructions fly out of your head, and you whirl your wheel *away* from the curb instead of *toward* it, and so you go sprawling on that granite-bound inhospitable shore. That was my luck; that was my experience. I dragged myself out from under the indestructible bicycle and sat down on the curb to examine.

I started on the return trip. It was now that I saw a
farmer's wagon poking along down toward me, loaded with
cabbages. If I needed anything to perfect the precariousness
of my steering, it was just that. The farmer was occupying
the middle of the road with his wagon, leaving barely
fourteen or fifteen yards of space on either side. I couldn't
shout at him—a beginner can't shout; if he opens his
mouth he is gone; he must keep all his attention on his
business. But in this grisly emergency, the boy came to the
rescue, and for once I had to be grateful to him. He kept a
sharp lookout on the swiftly varying impulses and
inspirations of my bicycle, and shouted to the man
accordingly:

"To the left. Turn to the left, or this jackass'll run over
you!" The man started to do it. "No, to the right, to the
right! Hold on! *that* won't do!—to the left!—to the
.right!—to the *left!*—right! left—ri—Stay where you *are*, or
you're a goner!"

And just then I caught the off horse in the starboard and
went down in a pile. I said, "Hang it! Couldn't you *see* I
was coming?"

"Yes, I see you was coming, but I couldn't tell which *way*
you was coming. Nobody could—now, *could* they? You
couldn't yourself—now, *could* you? So what could I do?"

There was something in that, and so I had the
magnanimity to say so. I said I was no doubt as much to
blame as he was.

Within the next five days I achieved so much progress
that the boy couldn't keep up with me. He had to go back
to his gate-post, and content himself with watching me fall
at long range.

There was a row of low stepping-stones across one end of
the street, a measured yard apart. Even after I got so I could

steer pretty fairly I was so afraid of those stones that I always hit them. They gave me the worst falls I ever got in that street, except those which I got from dogs. I have seen it stated that no expert is quick enough to run over a dog; that a dog is always able to skip out of his way. I think that that may be true: but I think that the reason he couldn't run over the dog was because he was trying to. I did not try to run over any dog. But I ran over every dog that came along. I think it makes a great deal of difference. If you try to run over the dog he knows how to calculate, but if you are trying to miss him he does not know how to calculate, and is liable to jump the wrong way every time. It was always so in my experience. Even when I could not hit a wagon I could hit a dog that came to see me practise. They all liked to see me practise, and they all came, for there was very little going on in our neighborhood to entertain a dog. It took time to learn to miss a dog, but I achieved even that.

I can steer as well as I want to, now, and I will catch that boy out one of these days and run over *him* if he doesn't reform.

Get a bicycle. You will not regret it, if you live.

INSCRIPTION FOR THE CEILING
OF A BEDROOM

Daily dawns another day;
I must up, to make my way.
Though I dress and drink and eat,
Move my fingers and my feet,
Learn a little, here and there,
Weep and laugh and sweat and swear,
Hear a song, or watch a stage,
Leave some words upon a page,
Claim a foe, or hail a friend—
Bed awaits me at the end.

Though I go in pride and strength,
I'll come back to bed at length.
Though I walk in blinded woe,
Back to bed I'm bound to go.
High my heart, or bowed my head,
All my days but lead to bed.
Up, and out, and on; and then
Ever back to bed again,
Summer, Winter, Spring, and Fall—
I'm a fool to rise at all!

DOROTHY PARKER

DON'T TAKE TOMORROW TO BED WITH YOU

I knew a man who complained of being a poor sleeper. We analyzed his daily and nightly habits and discovered that after he got to bed he took a pad and pencil and made a series of notes about what he was going to do the next day. He planned out tomorrow, making an outline of each problem or responsibility that was to be handled.

He prided himself on this "efficiency" method which he had developed, and considered it a unique procedure.

He placed the pen and pencil on his night table and would often reach for them in the darkness, adding additional memos that his restless mind supplied. He told with pride how well he had mastered the skill of writing legibly in the darkness.

Why couldn't he sleep? Simply because he was taking tomorrow to bed with him.

We, too, believe in efficiency. In fact one of our mottoes is, "plan your work and work your plan." But there is a time and place for all things, and in bed, ready to go to sleep, is certainly not the time to plan the next day. In fact, it is not efficient to do any tomorrow planning later than 9:00 P.M. if you are going to bed at 11:00 P.M.; not later than 8:00 P.M. if you are going to bed at 10:00 P.M. This interval of two hours will give the plans time to pass from the surface of the mind, where they agitate, into the deeper levels, where they become creative.

If, in sleeplessness, apprehensions of the morrow disturb you, simply remind yourself that God has helped you through every day you have lived heretofore, and that tomorrow will be no

exception. Slowly repeat aloud the following line from an old hymn: "So long Thy power has blest me, sure it still will lead me on." This will convince you of God's continuing care, and thus a comforted, relaxed feeling will come.

Also repeat this passage: "Sufficient unto the day is the evil thereof." (Matthew 6:34.)

That is to say, do not concern yourself about any presumed evil thing that may happen, for if that feared day comes, it will either care for itself, or you will know how to deal with it, or God will handle it. Certainly do not take it to bed with you and let it disturb your night's sleep, for nothing can be done about it tonight.

The happy fact is that what seems to you to presage evil may very well turn out to be good. At any rate, go to sleep in the conscious thought and affirmation that whatever you may be called upon to handle the next day, God and you can and will do together. Anyway, a good night's sleep will serve to muster needed powers to meet tomorrow's responsibilities. Relax in God's protecting care. In faith and trust let God give you rest. Remember that all things work together for good to those who love and trust God.

Don't take tomorrow to bed with you.

NORMAN VINCENT PEALE

PRAIRIE EVENING

That was a wonderful supper. They sat by the camp fire and ate the tender, savory, flavory meat till they could eat no more. When at last Laura set down her plate, she sighed with contentment. She didn't want anything more in the world.

The last color was fading from the enormous sky and all the level land was shadowy. The warmth of the fire was pleasant because the night wind was cool. Phoebe-birds called sadly from the woods down by the creek. For a little while a mockingbird sang, then the stars came out and the birds were still.

Softly Pa's fiddle sang in the starlight. Sometimes he sang a little and sometimes the fiddle sang alone. Sweet and thin and far away, the fiddle went on singing:

"None knew thee but to love thee,
Thou dear one of my heart. . . ."

The large, bright stars hung down from the sky. Lower and lower they came, quivering with music.

Laura gasped, and Ma came quickly. "What is it, Laura?" she asked, and Laura whispered, "The stars were singing."

"You've been asleep," Ma said. "It is only the fiddle. And it's time little girls were in bed."

She undressed Laura in the firelight and put her nightgown on and tied her nightcap, and tucked her into bed. But the fiddle was still singing in the starlight. The night was full of music, and Laura was sure that part of it came from the great, bright stars swinging so low above the prairie.

LAURA INGALLS WILDER

FLIGHT OF BIRDS

Watching the patterns of these birds in flight,
Fluid as music on a page and white
As falling petals, I find swift escape.
Then all at once my life takes sudden shape,
And I can understand the misprized art
Of reading palms or tea leaves in a cup;
Remember wise men searching in the skies,
Looking for omens in the tracks of birds,
Telling the future in cloud-darkened lines.

It is not fate in these external signs
We read; it is ourselves—ourselves we see,
Transmuted into bird or cloud or tree,
Familiar fragments, here arranged in form;
As a kaleidoscope contains the power
From common specks and straws to make a flower.

Act of creation in which the stone,
The sculptor, and the spectator, are one—
Here, where the art and artist coincide,
Where universe and private world collide,
Magic of mandala and Rorschach meet;
And childhood memories again repeat
Who loses life shall gain it—Miracle
The heart reborn upon a flight of birds
Can now accept and recognize in words.

ANNE MORROW LINDBERGH

FERN HILL

Now as I was young and easy under the apple boughs
About the lilting house and happy as the grass was green,
      The night above the dingle starry,
         Time let me hail and climb
      Golden in the heydays of his eyes,
And honoured among wagons I was prince of the apple towns
And once below a time I lordly had the trees and leaves
         Trail with daisies and barley
      Down the rivers of the windfall light.

And as I was green and carefree, famous among the barns
About the happy yard and singing as the farm was home,
      In the sun that is young once only,
         Time let me play and be
      Golden in the mercy of his means,
And green and golden I was huntsman and herdsman, the
              calves
Sang to my horn, the foxes on the hills barked clear and cold,
         And the sabbath rang slowly
      In the pebbles of the holy streams.

All the sun long it was running, it was lovely, the hay
Fields high as the house, the tunes from the chimneys, it
            was air
      And playing, lovely and watery
         And fire green as grass.
      And nightly under the simple stars
As I rode to sleep the owls were bearing the farm away,
All the moon long I heard, blessed among stables, the night-
            jars
      Flying with the ricks, and the horses
        Flashing into the dark.

And then to awake, and the farm, like a wanderer white
With the dew, come back, the cock on his shoulder: it was all
      Shining, it was Adam and maiden,
         The sky gathered again
      And the sun grew round that very day.
So it must have been after the birth of the simple light
In the first, spinning place, the spellbound horses walking
              warm
Out of the whinnying green stable
      On to the fields of praise.

And honoured among foxes and pheasants by the gay house
Under the new made clouds and happy as the heart was long,
      In the sun born over and over,
        I ran my heedless ways,
      My wishes raced through the house high hay
And nothing I cared, at my sky blue trades, that time allows
In all his tuneful turning so few and such morning songs
      Before the children green and golden
      Follow him out of grace,

Nothing I cared, in the lamb white days, that time would
         take me
Up to the swallow thronged loft by the shadow of my hand,
      In the moon that is always rising,
        Nor that riding to sleep
      I should hear him fly with the high fields
And wake to the farm forever fled from the childless land.
Oh as I was young and easy in the mercy of his means,
      Time held me green and dying
Though I sang in my chains like the sea.

DYLAN THOMAS

BIRD MAN

John James Audubon, the great naturalist painter, for years denied himself his true talent. He tried to be many things besides an artist, in order to support his wife, Lucy, and their children. Finally he broke loose—with Lucy's support—and followed his heart. This moving description by Donald Culross Peattie tells how Audubon set out "freed of that peculiar dishonor suffered by those who live lives for which they were never intended."

So he sailed into the morning of his adventure. All the birds of America were bound south upon their great autumnal flight, the plovers and the loons and ducks first to escape the oncoming arctic winter, the ibises and herons and whooping cranes lingering still in the balm of the days and the warmth of the brown waters. Now all that tropic crew, orioles, tanagers and chats, were on the wing, but many birds still called as if asking them why they went, those fleeting insect-eaters, those bright of wing and brave only in fair weather. At times, as if fear had suddenly overtaken them, there would band together for courage a flight of swifts or nighthawks or a long preposterous defile of pelicans. They passed John Audubon with a rush of wings in the night; they trailed against the yellow sinking moon. And by day the little warblers blew like a scattered shower through the falling leaves in the woods, and after them, picking up the crumbs of the year, came the first little snowbirds and juncos like flakes from the clouds in the north.

The flatboat reached the Mississippi, and turning due south now, Audubon had his back to winter. He was going, as the birds went, with the light, to the warmth. Life dealing with him more gently every day. Pines on the hills, the river looping in great oxbow bends. Blue-green islands, festooned with lianas. The first magnolias with their scarlet fruits above a glittering evergreen breadth of leaf; November roses around old houses with deep verandas and thin columns double-storied in height. Wine-red bayous lost to some stagnant enchantment of their own ... At Natchez, holes in his boots, and a cobbler who would shoe him for a portrait. Fresh game for the boat's whole company, and so, at the river's lazy gait, Louisiana at last, the French language, live-oaks and Spanish moss and birds that he had never seen before.

For Louisiana even in winter is as blessed with birds as many a northern land in summer; it is the permanent home of so many creatures of the air who know no reason that they should ever leave it; it is the winter solace of so many others. Its bird life has a strong tinge of the tropic. Audubon saw black vultures walking in the streets, as in any Mexican village; the chuck-will's-widow called in the woods; ground doves were feeding on the rice standing in its pale flooded fields. On the bayous the pelicans yawned monstrously, and the roseate flamingos thrust snaky necks among the water weeds.

Sheet by sheet, the bird drawings were filling the portfolio. When there should be enough of them, and every one of them satisfied him, he would try, he had determined, to publish them. This was now the single aim and hope of his existence. It was well that he had no conception of the difficulties, the costs, and the rebuffs in his path. He had no idea of the politics of publishing, or those of art and of science. That his ambition was absurd there were many people to tell him. But he believed in himself now and Lucy believed in him. All his life he had been helped, and generously helped, by her people and his own, to be something that he was not. And he had lost all that had been given him. He was flung stripped upon his own resources. He was left alone with himself to look at the quality of man he was. A dreamer? Yes, a dreamer who had come awake to find that the dream was true. From this point on—and we have the journals he now kept, to prove it—there is no wavering in the man; no one can shake him.

GREAT EXPECTATIONS

So long as people do not persuade themselves they are creatures of failure; so long as they have a vision of life as it ought to be; so long as they comprehend the full meaning and power of the unfettered mind—so long as this is so, they can look at the world and, beyond that, the universe with the sense that they can be unafraid of their fellow humans and can face choices not with dread but with great expectations.

NORMAN COUSINS

MAN IS A CONTRADICTION

Most thoughtful people recognize that man is a paradox. He is both dust of earth and breath of God. He is a contradiction of discord and harmony, hatred and love, pride and humility, tolerance and intolerance, and peace and turmoil. The depths to which he sinks only dramatize the heights to which by God's grace he is capable of rising. His very misery is an indication of his potential greatness. His deep yearnings are an echo of what he might be.

BILLY GRAHAM

God is our refuge and strength, a very present help in
trouble.
Therefore we will not fear though the earth should
change, though the mountains shake in the heart of the
sea;
though its waters roar and foam, though the mountains
tremble with its tumult.   *Selah*

There is a river whose streams make glad the city of
God, the holy habitation of the Most High.
God is in the midst of her, she shall not be moved; God
will help her right early.
The nations rage, the kingdoms totter; he utters his
voice, the earth melts.
The Lord of hosts is with us; the God of Jacob is our
refuge.   *Selah*

Come, behold the works of the Lord, how he has wrought
desolations in the earth.
He makes wars cease to the end of the earth; he breaks
the bow, and shatters the spear, he burns the chariots
with·fire!
"Be still, and know that I am God. I am exalted among
the nations, I am exalted in the earth!"
The Lord of hosts is with us; the God of Jacob is our
refuge.   *Selah*

PSALM 46

The Lord is my shepherd, I shall not want;
he makes me lie down in green pastures. He leads me be-
side still waters; he restores my soul.
He leads me in paths of righteousness for his name's sake.

Even though I walk through the valley of the shadow of
death, I fear no evil; for thou art with me; thy rod
and thy staff, they comfort me.

Thou preparest a table before me in the presence of my
enemies; thou anointest my head with oil, my cup over-
flows.

Surely goodness and mercy shall follow me all the days
of my life; and I shall dwell in the house of the Lord
for ever.

PSALM 23

ON SUCCESS AND FAILURE

A man who fails well is greater than one who succeeds badly.

One who is content with what he has, and who accepts the fact that he inevitably misses very much in life, is far better off than one who has much more but who worries about all he may be missing. For we cannot make the best of what we are, if our hearts are always divided between what we are and what we are not.

The lower our estimate of ourselves and the lower our expectations, the greater chance we have of using what we have. If we do not know how poor we are we will never be able to appreciate what we actually have. But, above all, we must learn our own weakness in order to awaken to a new order of action and of being—and experience God Himself accomplishing in us the things we find impossible.

We cannot be happy if we expect to live all the time at the highest peak of intensity. Happiness is not a matter of intensity but of balance and order and rhythm and harmony.

Music is pleasing not only because of the sound but because of the silence that is in it: without the alternation of sound and silence there would be no rhythm. If we strive to be happy by filling all the silences of life with sound, productive by turning all life's leisure into work, and real by turning all our being into doing, we will only succeed in producing a hell on earth.

If we have no silence, God is not heard in our music. If we have no rest, God does not bless our work. If we twist our lives out of shape in order to fill every corner of them with action and experience, God will silently withdraw from our hearts and leave us empty.

Let us, therefore, learn to pass from one imperfect activity to another without worrying too much about what we are missing. It is true that we make many mistakes. But the biggest of them all is to be surprised at them: as if we had some hope of never making any.

Mistakes are part of our life, and not the least important part. If we are humble, and if we believe in the Providence of God, we will see that our mistakes are not merely a necessary evil, something we must lament and count as lost: they enter into the very structure of our existence. It is by making mistakes that we gain experience, not only for ourselves but for others. And though our experience prevents neither ourselves nor others from making the same mistake many times, the repeated experience still has a positive value.

THOMAS MERTON

TELL HIM SO

If you hear a kind word spoken
  Of some worthy soul you know,
It may fill his heart with sunshine
  If you only tell him so.

If a deed, however humble,
  Helps you on your way to go,
Seek the one whose hand has helped you,
  Seek him out and tell him so!

If your heart is touched and tender
  Toward a sinner, lost and low,
It might help him to do better
  If you'd only tell him so!

Oh, my sisters, oh, my brothers,
  As o'er life's rough path you go,
If God's love has saved and kept you,
  Do not fail to tell men so!

AUTHOR UNKNOWN

ON CROSSING A STREAM BEFORE YOU REACH IT

Many years ago, when I was a young lawyer, and Illinois was little settled, except on her southern border, I, and other lawyers, used to ride the circuit; journeying with the judge from county-seat to county-seat in quest of business. Once, after a long spell of pouring rain, which had flooded the whole country, transforming small creeks into rivers, we were often stopped by these swollen streams, which we with difficulty crossed. Still ahead of us was the Fox River, larger than all the rest; and we could not help saying to each other, "If these streams give us so much trouble, how shall we get over Fox River?" Darkness fell before we had reached that stream; and we all stopped at a log tavern, had our horses put out, and resolved to pass the night. Here we were right glad to fall in with the Methodist Presiding Elder of the circuit, who rode it in all weather, knew all its ways, and could tell us about Fox River. So we all gathered around him, and asked him if he knew about the crossing of Fox River. "Oh, yes," he replied, "I know all about Fox River. I have crossed it often and understand it well; but I have one fixed rule with regard to Fox River: I never cross it till I reach it."

ABRAHAM LINCOLN

ON YOUTH AND AGE

The true test of maturity is not how old a person is but how he reacts to awakening in the midtown area in his shorts. What do years matter, particularly if your apartment is rent-controlled? The thing to remember is that each time of life has its appropriate rewards, whereas when you're dead it's hard to find the light switch. The chief problem about death, incidentally, is the fear that there may be no afterlife—a depressing thought, particularly for those who have bothered to shave. Also, there is the fear that there is an afterlife but no one will know where it's being held. On the plus side, death is one of the few things that can be done as easily lying down.

Consider, then: Is old age really so terrible? Not if you've brushed your teeth faithfully! And why is there no buffer to the onslaught of the years? Or a good hotel in downtown Indianapolis? Oh, well.

In short, the best thing to do is behave in a manner befitting one's age. If you are sixteen or under, try not to go bald. On the other hand, if you are over eighty, it is extremely good form to shuffle down the street clutching a brown paper bag and muttering, "The Kaiser will steal my string." Remember, everything is relative—or should be. If it's not, we must begin again.

WOODY ALLEN

BEN FRANKLIN'S RULES FOR IMPROVING HIS BEHAVIOR

1. Temperance: Eat not to dullness; drink not to elevation.
2. Silence: Speak not but what may benefit others or yourself; avoid trifling conversation.
3. Order: Let all your things have their places; let each part of your business have its time.
4. Resolution: Resolve to perform what you ought; perform without fail what you resolve.
5. Frugality: Make no expense but to do good to others or yourself; *i.e.*, waste nothing.
6. Industry: Lose no time; be always employed in something useful; cut off all unnecessary actions.
7. Sincerity: Use no hurtful deceit; think innocently and justly; and if you speak, speak accordingly.
8. Justice: Wrong none by doing injuries, or omitting the benefits that are your duty.
9. Moderation: Avoid extremes; forbear resenting injuries so much as you think they deserve.
10. Cleanliness: Tolerate no uncleanliness in body, clothes, or habitation.
11. Tranquility: Be not disturbed at trifles, or at accidents common or unavoidable.
12. Chastity.
13. Humility: Imitate Jesus and Socrates.

GOING TO BED WITH MUSIC

Half our days we pass in the shadow of the earth; and the brother of death exacteth a third part of our lives. A good part of our sleep is peered out with visions and fantastical objects, wherein we are confessedly deceived. The day supplieth us with truth; the night with fictions and falsehoods which uncomfortably divide the natural account of our beings. And, therefore, having passed the day in sober labours and rational enquiries of truth, we are fain to betake ourselves unto such a state of being, wherein the soberest heads have acted all the monstrosities of melancholy, and which unto open eyes are no better than folly and madness.

Happy are they that go to bed with grand music, like Pythagoras, or have ways to compose the fantastical spirit, whose unruly wanderings take off inward sleep, filling our heads with St. Anthony's visions, and the dreams of Lipara in the sober chamber of rest.

SIR THOMAS BROWNE

AFTERNOON ON A HILL

I will be the gladdest thing
   Under the sun!
I will touch a hundred flowers
   And not pick one.

I will look at cliffs and clouds
   With quiet eyes,
Watch the wind bow down the grass,
   And the grass rise.

And when lights begin to show
   Up from the town,
I will mark which must be mine,
   And then start down!

EDNA ST. VINCENT MILLAY

A THING OF BEAUTY

A thing of beauty is a joy for ever:
Its loveliness increases; it will never
Pass into nothingness; but still will keep
A bower quiet for us, and a sleep
Full of sweet dreams, and health, and quiet breathing.
Therefore, on every morrow, are we wreathing
A flowery band to bind us to the earth,
Spite of despondence, of the inhuman dearth
Of noble natures, of the gloomy days,
Of all the unhealthy and o'er-darkened ways
Made for our searching: yes, in spite of all,
Some shape of beauty moves away the pall
From our dark spirits. Such the sun, the moon,
Trees old and young, sprouting a shady boon
For simple sheep; and such are daffodils

With the green world they live in; and clear rills
That for themselves a cooling covert make
'Gainst the hot season; the mid-forest brake,
Rich with a sprinkling of fair musk-rose blooms:
And such too is the grandeur of the dooms
We have imagined for the mighty dead;
All lovely tales that we have heard or read:
An endless fountain of immortal drink,
Pouring unto us from the heaven's brink.
Nor do we merely feel these essences
For one short hour; no, even as the trees
That whisper round a temple become soon
Dear as the temple's self, so does the moon,
The passion poesy, glories infinite,
Haunt us till they become a cheering light
Unto our souls, and bound to us so fast,
That, whether there be shine, or gloom o'ercast,
They always must be with us, or we die.

JOHN KEATS

A VISIT FROM THE SEA

Far from the loud sea beaches
    Where he goes fishing and crying,
Here in the inland garden
    Why is the seagull flying?

Here are no fish to dive for;
    Here is the corn and lea;
Here are the green trees rustling.
    Hie away home to sea!

Fresh is the river water
    And quiet among the rushes;
This is no home for the seagull
    But for the rooks and thrushes.

Pity the bird that has wandered!
    Pity the sailor ashore!
Hurry him home to the ocean,
    Let him come here no more!

High on the seacliff ledges
    The white gulls are trooping and crying,
Here among rooks and roses,
    Why is the seagull flying?

ROBERT LOUIS STEVENSON

WORLD FOREVER NEW

Consider that the perpetual admonition of Nature to us is, The world is new, untried. Do not believe in the past. I give you the universe new and unhandled every hour. You think in your idle hours that there is literature, history, science behind you so accumulated as to exhaust thought and prescribe your own future and the future. In your sane hour you shall see that not a line has yet been written; that for all the poetry that is in the world your first sensation on entering a wood or standing on the shore of a lake has not been chanted yet. It remains for you, so does all thought, all object, all life remain unwritten still.

RALPH WALDO EMERSON

LIFE

We justify the gift of life in many ways—by our awareness of its preciousness and its fragility; by developing to the fullest the sensitivities and potentialities that come with life; by putting the whole of our intelligence to work in sustaining and enhancing the conditions that make life possible; by cherishing the human habitat and shielding it from devastation and depletion; by removing the obstructions in our access to, and trust in, one another.

NORMAN COUSINS

THE POLAR-NIGHT

. . . the coming of the polar night is not the spectacular rush that some imagine it to be. The day is not abruptly walled off; the night does not drop suddenly. Rather, the effect is a gradual accumulation, like that of an infinitely prolonged tide. Each day the darkness, which is the tide, washes in a little farther and stays a little longer; each time the day, which is a beach, contracts a little more, until at last it is covered. The onlooker is not conscious of haste. On the contrary, he is sensible of something of incalculable importance being accomplished with timeless patience. The going of the day is a gradual process, modulated by the intervention of twilight. You look up, and it is gone. But not completely. Long after the horizon has interposed itself, the sun continues to cast up a pale and dwindling imitation of the day. You can trace its progress by the glow thrown up as it makes its round just below the horizon.

These are the best times, the times when neglected senses expand to an exquisite sensitivity. You stand on the Barrier, and simply look and listen and feel. The morning may be compounded of an unfathomable, tantalizing fog in which you stumble over sastrugi you can't see, and detour past obstructions that don't exist, and take your bearings from tiny bamboo markers that loom as big as telephone poles and hang suspended in space. On such a day, I could swear that the instrument shelter was as big as an ocean liner. On one such day I saw the blank northeastern sky become filled with the most magnificent Barrier coast I have ever seen, true in every line and faced with cliffs several thousand feet tall. A mirage, of course. Yet, a man who had never seen such things would have taken oath that it was real. The afternoon may be so clear that you dare not make a sound, lest it fall in pieces. And on

such a day I have seen the sky shatter like a broken goblet, and dissolve into iridescent tipsy fragments—ice crystals falling across the face of the sun. And once in the golden downpour a slender column of platinum leaped up from the horizon, clean through the sun's core; a second luminous shadow formed horizontally through the sun, making a perfect cross. Presently two miniature suns, green and yellow in color, flipped simultaneously to the ends of each arm. These are parhelia, the most dramatic of all refraction phenomena; nothing is lovelier.

RICHARD E. BYRD

A MIDSUMMER'S NIGHT'S STORM

Night, Lightning, Thunder, Rain.
    I see black Night
Open her lips;
    Her teeth gleam bright,
A moment seen;
    Then comes rich laughter;
And happy tears,
    That follow after,
Fall on the bosoms
Of birds and blossoms.

W. H. DAVIES

PRAYER

Shepherd who dost not sleep, keep watch and ward over thy flock of souls.

Amen.

And that it be not disturbed by terror of the night, sanctify it by the unseen touch of thy hand.

Amen.

Make the frail stalwart, lift up the contrite, make the weak strong. Raise up by piety, build up by charity, purify by chastity, illuminate by wisdom, save by pity.

Amen.

Let watchful faith win the reward of constancy in thy love, temperance of habit, providence in mercy, discipline of conduct.

Amen.

In thy merciful compassion shut not out from the splendour of thy promise, but lead to pardon, him whom thou hast made thine own by grace.

Amen.

GOTHIC MISSAL

THE GOLDEN RULE

Mahabharata, c. 800 B.C.: Deal with others as thou wouldst thyself be dealt by. Do nothing to thy neighbor which thou wouldst not have him to thee hereafter.

Dadistan-I dinik, Zend-Avesta, c. 700 B.C.: That nature only is good when it shall not do unto another whatever is not good for its own self.

Undana Varga, c. 500 B.C.: Hurt not others with that which pains yourself.

Confucius, c. 400 B.C.: Tuan-mu Tzv said, "What I do not wish others to do unto me I also wish not to do unto others." Do not unto others what you would not they should do unto you.

Panchatantra, c. 200 B.C.: Ponder well the maxim: Never do to other persons what would pain thyself.

Hillel Ha-Babli, c. 30 B.C.: Whatsoever thou wouldst that men should not do to thee, do not do that to them. This is the whole law. The rest is only explanation.

Mohammed, c. A.D. 600: Say not, if people are good to us, we will do good to them, and if people oppress us we will oppress them: but resolve that if people do good to you, you will do good to them, and if they oppress you, oppress them not again.

ON FIRST LOOKING INTO CHAPMAN'S HOMER

Much have I travelled in the realms of gold,
    And many goodly states and kingdoms seen;
    Round many western islands have I been
Which bards in fealty to Apollo hold.
Oft of one wide expanse had I been told
    That deep-browed Homer ruled as his demesne:
    Yet did I never breathe its pure serene
Till I heard Chapman speak out loud and bold:
Then felt I like some watcher of the skies
    When a new planet swims into his ken;
Or like stout Cortez, when with eagle eyes
    He stared at the Pacific—and all his men
Looked at each other with a wild surmise—
    Silent, upon a peak in Darien.

JOHN KEATS

THE OPENING WORLD

When I was eleven years old, I heard the cello played for the first time. That was the beginning of a long and cherished companionship! A trio had come to play at a concert in Vendrell—a pianist, a violinist and a cellist. My father took me to the concert. It was held at the small hall of the Catholic Center, with an audience of townspeople, fishermen and peasants, who, as always for such an occasion, were dressed in their Sunday clothes. The cellist was Josep García, a teacher at the Municipal School of Music in Barcelona; he was a handsome man with a high forehead and a handlebar mustache; and his figure somehow seemed fitted to his instrument. When I saw his cello I was fascinated by it—I had never seen one before. From the moment I heard the first notes I was overwhelmed. I felt as if I could not breathe. There was something so tender, beautiful and human—yes, so very human—about the sound. I had never heard such a beautiful sound before. A radiance filled me. When the first composition was ended, I told my father, "Father, that is the most wonderful instrument I have ever heard. That is what I want to play."

After the concert I kept talking to my father about the cello, pleading with him to get me one. From that time, more than eighty years ago, I was wedded to the instrument. It would be my companion and friend for the rest of my life. I had of course found joy in the violin, the piano and other instruments, but for me the cello was something special and unique. I began playing my violin holding it like a cello.

My mother understood what had happened. She told my

father, "Pablo shows such enthusiasm for the cello that he must have the chance really to study it. There is no teacher here in Vendrell who is qualified to teach him properly. We must arrange for him to go to the School of Music in Barcelona."

My father was astonished. "What in the world are you talking about?" he asked. "How can Pablo possibly go to Barcelona? We simply do not have the money."

My mother said, "We will find a way. I will take him there. Pablo is a musician. This is his nature. This is what he was made to be. He must go anywhere necessary. There is no other choice."

My father was not at all convinced—he was, in fact, already thinking about my following the trade of a carpenter in order to earn a living. "You have delusions of grandeur," he told my mother.

Their discussions on the subject became more and more frequent and intense. It troubled me greatly. I felt I was to blame for the disagreement between them. I asked myself how I could end it, but I didn't know what to do. Finally, my father reluctantly gave in. He wrote a letter to the Municipal School of Music in Barcelona asking if they would accept me as a pupil. He also said that I would need a small cello, three-quarter size, and asked if they knew an instrument maker who could make one for me.

Even so, after the school had responded favorably and as the time approached for my going to Barcelona, my father continued to express misgivings.

"Dear Carlos," my mother would tell him, "you may be sure that this is right. This is what has to be. It is the only thing for Pablo."

My father would shake his head. "I do not understand, I do not understand."

And she would say, "I know that, but you must have faith. You must be confident; you must."

It was a truly remarkable thing. My mother had had some musical training, but she was not of course a musician in the sense my father was. Yet she knew what my future was to be. She had known, I believe, from the beginning; it was as if she had some special sensitivity, a peculiar prescience. She knew; and she always acted on the knowledge with a firmness and certainty and calmness that has never ceased to amaze me. This was so not only about my studying in Barcelona, but in later years, on other occasions when I was at a crossroads in my career. It was so also with my younger brothers, Luis and Enrique; when they were still children, she knew the paths that they would follow. And later when I was playing concerts in many parts of the world and some success had come to me, she was happy but I would not say impressed. She had assumed this would be so.

During my life I myself have come to understand what she believed. I have come to the feeling that what happens must happen. I do not mean of course that there is nothing we can do about what we are or what we shall become. Everything about us is in a constant state of change—that is the way of nature; and we ourselves are changing all the time, for we are part of nature. We have the duty always to work to change ourselves for the better. But I do believe we have our destinies.

PABLO CASALS

YOUTH

Youth is not a time of life; it is a state of mind, it is not a
matter of rosy cheeks, red lips and supple knees; it is a
matter of the will, a quality of the imagination, a vigor of
the emotions; it is the freshness of the deep springs of life.

Youth means the temperamental predominance of courage over
timidity of the appetite, for adventure over the love of
ease. This often exists in a man of sixty more than a boy
of twenty. Nobody grows old merely by a number of
years. We grow old by deserting our ideals.

Years may wrinkle the skin, but to give up enthusiasm wrinkles
the soul. Worry, fear, self-distrust bows the heart and turns
the spirit back to dust.

Whether sixty or sixteen, there is in every human being's heart
the lure of wonder, the unfailing child-like appetite of
what's next, and the joy of the game of living. In the
center of your heart and my heart there is a wireless
station; so long as it receives messages of beauty, hope,
cheer, courage and power from men and from the Infinite,
so long are you young.

When the aerials are down, and your spirit is covered with
snows of cynicism and the ice of pessimism, then you are
grown old, even at twenty, but as long as your aerials are
up, to catch waves of optimism; there is hope you may die
young at eighty.

SAMUEL ULLMAN

OLD ENGLISH PRAYER

Take time to work—
    It is the price of success.
Take time to think—
    It is the source of power.
Take time to play—
    It is the secret of perpetual youth.
Take time to read—
    It is the fountain of wisdom.
Take time to be friendly—
    It is the road to happiness.
Take time to dream—
    It is hitching your wagon to a star.
Take time to love and to be loved—
    It is the privilege of the gods.
Take time to look around—
    It is too short a day to be selfish.
Take time to laugh—
    It is the music of the soul.

AUTHOR UNKNOWN

LET NO JOB BE BENEATH ME

Thank you, God, for the wonderful gift of work. Humble work. Hard work. Brain work or back work or hand work.

I don't care much for lily-white brains and lily-white hands. I like brains that have been toughened and tried. I like backs that have been strengthened and even bent by their burdens.

I like hands that are tough, too—wrinkled from water, calloused and bruised from rocks and shovels and hammer and nails. I like hands and backs and brains that have wrestled with things, lifted and carried.

Thank you that my parents worked hard and taught their children to work hard.

Help me to remember that no job is beneath me, and with your help no job will be beyond me.

MARJORIE HOLMES

WORK

Let me but do my work from day to day,
In field or forest, at the desk or loom,
In roaring market-place or tranquil room;
Let me but find it in my heart to say,
When vagrant wishes beckon me astray,
"This is my work; my blessing, not my doom;
Of all who live, I am the one by whom
This work can best be done in the right way."

Then shall I see it not too great, nor small
To suit my spirit and to prove my powers;
Then shall I cheerful greet the laboring hours,
And cheerful turn, when the long shadows fall
At eventide, to play and love and rest,
Because I know for me my work is best.

HENRY VAN DYKE

From SONG OF THE OPEN ROAD

Afoot and light-hearted, I take to the open road,
Healthy, free, the world before me,
The long brown path before me, leading wherever I choose.

Henceforth I ask not good fortune—I myself am good-fortune;
Henceforth I whimper no more, postpone no more, need
    nothing,
Strong and content, I travel the open road. . . .

From this hour, freedom!
From this hour I ordain myself loos'd of limits and imaginary
    lines,
Going where I list, my own master, total and absolute,
Listening to others, and considering well what they say,
Pausing, searching, receiving, contemplating,
Gently, but with undeniable will, divesting myself, of the holds
    that would hold me.

I inhale great draughts of space;
The east and the west are mine, and the north and the south
    are mine.

I am larger, better than I thought;
I did not know I held so much goodness.
All seems beautiful to me;
I can repeat over to men and women, You have done such
    good to me, I would do the same to you.

I will recruit for myself and you as I go;
I will scatter myself among men and women as I go;
I will toss the new gladness and roughness among them;
Whoever denies me, it shall not trouble me;
Whoever accepts me, he or she shall be blessed, and shall bless
    me. . . .

WALT WHITMAN

ALONG THE RIVER

The moon was just coming over the tree tops, and the shadows were thick and dark. A dog began to bark as we passed the little village and walked back along the river. The river was so still that it caught the stars and the lights of the long bridge among its waters. High up on the bank children were standing and laughing, and a baby was crying. The fishermen were cleaning and coiling their nets. A night-bird flew silently by. Someone began to sing on the other bank of the wide river, and his words were clear and penetrating. Again the all-pervading aloneness of life.

J. KRISHNAMURTI

WAVES

I lay under the low yellow cliff, on a bank of shingle facing the sea.

It was October. All night a new unfriendly gale had rattled our windows; in the morning trees looked harassed, and leaves, speckled, as though they had the plague, whirled distractedly at street corners.

The sea had a far, wide look; brown and grey shadows lay across it from the wave's edge to the horizon.

One had seen the tide slip in and out, gently running up and down the sands all through September, but suddenly I made the discovery that the body of the sea moved. There was a thin silver flash on the far edge—a line of indigo—that rose up into a dazzle of light with each fresh wave; the whole energy of that mass of water was drawn up into a long wall that curved and brimmed and rolled over flat wastes of foam; that was pushed on irresistibly.

When it broke in thunder, my heart leaped. Happy the sun-sparkles that can play like reflections of a white furnace upon it.

I watched lather, like soap-suds, dashed on to dead-looking, sea-weed banks, that came to life in the contact, with wet brown shadows, and blowing ribbons of amber. One felt that disease must perish, if all the sick could be laid at the edge of the waves, with this salt, fresh gale in their faces.

Baby was with me, her little red cloak peaked like a hobgoblin's. With quite fearless, unspeculative eyes she looked at the water, her attention absorbed in finding "mermaid's purses."

She felt, without thinking, that the sea had its bounds; and the angry colour, that to me was indicative of its spirit, was sand stirred up and lights from the storm clouds. The waves were "white horses," and the fact of the great sea, fresh and thundering forever, lay in her quiet child's balance as something infinitely less than herself. So she stooped with her back to it—searching for "mermaid's purses" in the sea-weed.

But the wonder of waves had gone over me; the force of attraction which drew them to rise out of the level sea, and shatter themselves on stones; which caused that little after-ripple, and compelled the next wave.

The edge of the sea was black with weed, that floated on the oily swell stretching between, and was thrown up dark and heavy in the foam.

From far out one could watch the seventh wave, undulating along the top of the water; growing, rising, a line of darkness towering to a thin edge; then it sweeps the shadows before it; rolls, as though it were the depth of the sea risen up to the clouds.

One held one's breath; suddenly hollowed and curving, with yellow sunlight through its arching crest, unspeakable blackness in its trough, it topples forward, pulled by the force that had drawn it up—breaking, a foaming waterfall, thunder, wild horses plunging, and its wet reflection in the sea before it. A white waste of driven foam boiling over the black weed. Silence, but for its death-sigh effervescing into fresh life on the wind. And then the long wash back, with the rolling stones—to the sea.

DOROTHY EASTON

TRAVELLING-NOTES

The Kaatsberg, or Catskill Mountains, have always been a region full of fable. The Indians considered them the abode of spirits, who influenced the weather, spreading sunshine or clouds over the landscape, and sending good or bad hunting seasons. They were ruled by an old squaw spirit, said to be their mother. She dwelt on the highest peak of the Catskills, and had charge of the doors of day and night to open and shut them at the proper hour. She hung up the new moon in the skies, and cut up the old ones into stars. In times of drought, if properly propitiated, she would spin light summer clouds out of cobwebs and morning dew, and send them off from the crest of the mountain, flake after flake, like flakes of carded cotton, to float in the air; until, dissolved by the heat of the sun, they would fall in gentle showers, causing the grass to spring, the fruits to ripen, and the corn to grow an inch an hour. If displeased, however, she would brew up clouds black as ink, sitting in the midst of them like a bottle-bellied spider in the midst of its web; and when these clouds broke, woe betide the valleys!

In old times, say the Indian traditions, there was a kind of Manitou or Spirit, who kept about the wildest recesses of the Catskill Mountains and took a mischievous pleasure in wreaking all kinds of evils and vexations upon the red men. Sometimes he would assume the form of a bear, a panther, or a deer, lead the bewildered hunter a weary chase through tangled forests and among ragged rocks; and then spring off with a loud ho! ho! leaving him aghast on the brink of a beetling precipice or raging torrent.

The favourite abode of this Manitou is still shown. It is a great rock or cliff on the loneliest part of the mountains, and, from the flowering vines which clamber about it, and the wild flowers which abound in its neighbourhood, is known by the name of the Garden Rock. Near the foot of it is a small lake, the haunt of the solitary bittern, with watersnakes basking in the sun on the leaves of the pond-lilies which lie on the surface. This place was held in great awe by the Indians, insomuch that the boldest hunter would not pursue his game within its precincts. Once upon a time, however, a hunter, who had lost his way, penetrated to the Garden Rock, where he beheld a number of gourds placed in the crotches of trees. One of these he seized and made off with it, but in the hurry of his retreat he let it fall among the rocks, when a great stream gushed forth, which washed him away and swept him down precipices, where he was dashed to pieces, and the stream made its way to the Hudson, and continues to flow to the present day; being the identical stream known by the name of the Kaaterskill.

WASHINGTON IRVING

THE OWL AND THE PUSSY-CAT

The Owl and the Pussy-Cat went to sea
    In a beautiful pea-green boat.
They took some honey and plenty of money
    Wrapped up in a five-pound note.
The Owl looked up to the stars above,
    And sang to a small guitar,
"Oh lovely Pussy! O Pussy, my love!
    What a beautiful Pussy you are,—
        You are;
    What a beautiful Pussy you are!"

Pussy said to the Owl, "You elegant fowl,
    How charmingly sweet you sing!
Oh, let us be married,—too long we have tarried,—
    But what shall we do for a ring?"
They sailed away for a year and a day,
    To the land where the bong-tree grows;
And there, in a wood, a Piggy-wig stood,—
    With a ring at the end of his nose,
        His nose;
    With a ring at the end of his nose.

"Dear Pig, are you willing to sell for one shilling
    Your ring?" Said the Piggy, "I will."
So they took it away, and were married next day
    By the Turkey who lives on the hill.
They dined upon mince and slices of quince,
    Which they ate with a runcible spoon;
And hand in hand, on the edge of the sand,
    They danced by the light of the moon,—
        The moon;
    They danced by the light of the moon.

EDWARD LEAR

QUESTIONS AND ANSWERS

*A New York publisher sent Mark Twain a page of questions,
with blanks for answers, called a Mental Photograph Album.*

MARK TWAIN REPLIED—Nothing could induce me to fill
these blanks but the asservation of my pastor. This overcomes
my scruples.

I have but little character, but what I have I am willing to
part with for the public good.

I have filled the blanks as follows:

WHAT IS YOUR FAVORITE TREE?
   Any that bears forbidden fruit.
FAVORITE GEM?
   The Jack of Diamonds, when it is trump.
WHAT IS YOUR IDEA OF HAPPINESS?
   Finding the buttons all on.
WHAT DO YOU MOST DREAD?
   Exposure.
WHAT DO YOU BELIEVE TO BE YOUR DISTINGUISHING
CHARACTERISTIC?
   Hunger.
WHAT ARE THE SADDEST WORDS IN THE WORLD?
   "Dust unto dust."
WHAT ARE THE SWEETEST?
   Not guilty.
WHAT IS YOUR AIM IN LIFE?
   To endeavor to be absent when my time comes.
WHAT IS YOUR MOTTO?
   Be virtuous and you will be eccentric.

From A SLICE OF SUNLIGHT

In every man's heart there is a secret nerve that answers to the vibration of beauty. I can imagine no more fascinating privilege than to be allowed to ransack the desks of a thousand American business men, men supposed to be hardheaded, absorbed in brisk commerce. Somewhere in each desk one would find some hidden betrayal of that man's private worship. It might be some old newspaper clipping, perhaps a poem that had once touched him, for even the humblest poets are stout partisans of reality. It might be a photograph of children playing in the surf, or a little box of fishhooks, or a soiled old timetable of some queer backwoods railroad or primitive steamer service that had once carried him into his land of heart's desire.

I remember a friend of mine, a man much perplexed by the cares of earth, but slow to give utterance to his inner and tenderer impulses, telling me how he first grasped the meaning and value of these inscrutable powers of virtue that hurl the whole universe daily around our heads in an unerring orbit. For some reason or other—he was writing a book, I think, and sought a place of quiet—he had drifted for some winter weeks to the shore of a southern bay, down in Florida. When he came back he told me about it. It was several years ago, but I remember the odd look in his eyes as he tried to describe his experience. "I never knew until now," he said, "what sunshine

and sky meant. I had always taken them for granted before."
He told me of the strange sensation of lightness and quiet
smiling that had flooded through him in that land where
Nature writes her benignant lessons so plainly that all must
draw their own conclusions. He told me of sunset flushes over
long, purple waters, and of lying on sand beaches wrapped in
sunshine, all the problems of human intercourse soothed away
in a naked and unquestioning content. What he said was very
little, but watching his eyes I could guess what had happened.
He had found more than sunshine and colour and an arc of
violet sea. He had found a new philosophy, a new strength and
realization of the worthiness of life. He had travelled far to find
it: it might just as well be learned in Independence Square any
sunny day when the golden light falls upon springing grass.

It is strange that men should have to be reminded of these
things! How patiently, how persistently, with what dogged and
misdirected pluck, they have taught themselves to ignore the
elemental blessings of mankind, subsisting instead on pale and
wizened and ingenious substitutes. It is like a man who should
shoulder for a place at a quick lunch counter when a broad
and leisurely banquet table was spread free just around the
corner. The days tick by, as busy, as fleeting, as full of empty
gestures as a moving picture film. We crowd old age upon
ourselves and run out to embrace it, for age is not measured by
number of days but by the exhaustion of each day. Twenty
days lived at slow pulse, in harmony with earth's loveliness, are
longer than two hundred crowded with feverish appointments
and disappointments. Many a man has lived fifty or sixty
hectic years and never yet learned the unreckonable
endlessness of one day's loitering, measured only by the
gracious turning of earth and sun. Someone often asks me,

"Why don't you wind the clocks?" But in those rare moments when I am sane clocks do not interest me.

Something of these thoughts flashes into my mind as I see that beam of pale and narrow sunlight fallen upon the roof of that bank building. How strange it is, when life is bursting with light and strength, renewing itself every day in colour and freshness, that we should sunder ourselves from these great sources of power. With all the treasures of earth at hand, we coop ourselves in narrow causeways where even a sudden knife-edge of brightness is a matter for joyful surprise. As Stevenson once said, it is all very well to believe in immortality, but one must first believe in life. Why do we grudge ourselves the embraces of "Our brother and good friend the Sun"?

CHRISTOPHER MORLEY

WHAT IS ENOUGH?

Would that there were an award for people who come to understand the concept of enough. Good enough. Successful enough. Thin enough. Rich enough. Socially responsible enough. When you have self-respect, you have enough; and when you have enough, you have self-respect. Fortunately, because there are always people and events to stretch us, none of us needs worry about falling into the self-satisfied sloughs of "absolute" maturity.

It would be surprising if we didn't experience some pain as we leave the familiarity of one adult stage for the uncertainty of the next. But the willingness to move through each passage is equivalent to the willingness to live abundantly. If we don't change, we don't grow. If we don't grow, we are not really living. Growth demands a temporary surrender of security. It may mean a giving up of familiar but limiting patterns, safe but unrewarding work, values no longer believed in, relationships that have lost their meaning. As Dostoevsky put it, "taking a new step, uttering a new word, is what people fear most." The real fear should be of the opposite course.

If physical strength and pleasures of the senses are held to be life's greatest values, then we deny ourselves anything beyond youth but a dull ebb of all experience. If we see nothing to rival the accumulation of goods and success, then we trap ourselves into a stale and repetitious middle age. Yet the delights of self-discovery are always available. Though loved ones move in and out of our lives, the capacity to love remains. And for the mind freed of the constant strivings of earlier years, there is time in the later years to ponder the mysteries of existence without interruption.

GAIL SHEEHY

CONTRASTS

In her book, CHANGING, the highly-acclaimed actress Liv Ullmann writes of her impressions while in Norway on tour with Ibsen's "A Doll's House."

A Doll's House is on tour again. This time we are competing with the midnight sun in northern Norway. For a week I am unable to sleep because it is so beautiful there.

What a country I live in! Snow-capped mountains and the smell of heather and bog. A fresh breath of air from water that is pure, from fjords that wind into the strangest hidden places. Where in summer the sun never disappears, just kisses the horizon before it rises again and sets off on its journey across the sky.

People who spontaneously show what they are feeling, and talk in eager singing voices, as if they cannot get over their delight at being out of the eternal darkness of winter.

North Norway when the thermometer records ninety degrees and I lie naked on the bed without a quilt and the light beats on the windowpanes all night.

I have traveled all over the world, and I'm quite certain that for me no impressions have been stronger than those I experience now. The contrasts here are so immense. The sea so bottomless when I lean over a ship's rail and imagine all the adventure deep down in the water. The mountains towering over me on all sides, wild and barren, closer to heaven than I thought mountains could get.

To feel the wind and the sun on the face—and at the same time feel the fragrance of trees and rocks and the earth I walk on touch the skin—that is part of what changes my life.

A MEMORY

On overcast afternoons, all alone in the drizzle, my mother, carrying a basket (stained blue on the inside by somebody's whortleberries), would set out on a long collecting tour. Toward dinnertime, she could be seen emerging from the nebulous depths of a park alley, her small figure cloaked and hooded in greenish-brown wool, on which countless droplets of moisture made a kind of mist all around her. Just before reaching me, with an abrupt, drooping movement of the arm and shoulder and a "Pouf!" of magnified exhaustion, she would let her basket sag, in order to stress its weight, its fabulous fullness.

Near a white garden bench, on a round garden table of iron, she would lay out her boletes in concentric circles to count and sort them. Old ones, with spongy, dingy flesh, would be eliminated, leaving the young and the crisp. For a moment, before they were bundled away by a servant to a place she knew nothing about, to a doom that did not interest her, she would stand there admiring them, in a glow of quiet contentment. As often happened at the end of a rainy day, the sun might cast a lurid gleam just before setting, and there, on the damp round table, her mushrooms would lie, very colorful, some bearing traces of extraneous vegetation—a grass blade sticking to a viscid fawn cap, or moss still clothing the bulbous base of a dark-stippled stem. And a tiny looper caterpillar would be there, too, measuring, like a child's finger and thumb, the rim of the table, and every now and then stretching upward to grope, in vain, for the shrub from which it had been dislodged.

VLADIMIR NABOKOV

THE DAY IS DONE

The day is done, and the darkness
    Falls from the wings of Night,
As a feather is wafted downward
    From an eagle in his flight.

I see the lights of the village
    Gleam through the rain and the mist:
And a feeling of sadness comes o'er me,
    That my soul cannot resist:

A feeling of sadness and longing,
    That is not akin to pain,
And resembles sorrow only
    As the mist resembles the rain.

Come, read to me some poem,
    Some simple and heartfelt lay,
That shall soothe this restless feeling,
    And banish the thoughts of day.

Not from the grand old masters,
    Not from the bards sublime,
Whose distant footsteps echo
    Through the corridors of Time.

For, like strains of martial music,
    Their mighty thoughts suggest
Life's endless toil and endeavor;
    And to-night I long for rest.

Read from some humbler poet,
    Whose songs gush'd from his heart,
As showers from the clouds of summer,
    Or tears from the eyelids start;

Who, through long days of labor,
    And nights devoid of ease,
Still heard in his soul the music
    Of wonderful melodies.

Such songs have power to quiet
    The restless pulse of care,
And come like the benediction
    That follows after prayer.

Then read from the treasured volume
    The poem of thy choice;
And lend to the rhyme of the poet
    The beauty of thy voice.

And the night shall be fill'd with music,
    And the cares that infest the day
Shall fold their tents like the Arabs,
    And as silently steal away.

HENRY WADSWORTH LONGFELLOW

Acknowledgments

The editor and the publisher have made every effort to trace the ownership of all copyrighted material and to secure permission from copyright holders of such material. In the event of any question arising as to the use of any material the publisher and editor, while expressing regret for inadvertent error, will be pleased to make the necessary corrections in future printings. Thanks are due to the following authors, publishers, publications and agents for permission to use the material indicated.

NORMAN COUSINS, for an excerpt from "A Rendezvous With Infinity" by Norman Cousins as appeared in *Saturday Review/World* (February 9, 1974); for an excerpt from "Life Without Helplessness" by Norman Cousins as appeared in *Saturday Review/World* (December 4, 1973).

DOUBLEDAY & COMPANY, INC., for an excerpt from *Intuition* by R. Buckminster Fuller. Copyright © 1972 by R. Buckminster Fuller; for "Let No Job Be Beneath Me" from *How Can I Find You, God?* by Marjorie Holmes. Copyright © 1975 by Marjorie Holmes Mighell.

E. P. DUTTON & COMPANY, INC., for an excerpt from *Passages* by Gail Sheehy. Copyright © 1974, 1976 by Gail Sheehy.

BILLY GRAHAM EVANGELISTIC ASSOCIATION, for an excerpt from *Past, Present and Future* by Billy Graham. Copyright © 1958 by the Billy Graham Evangelistic Association.

HARCOURT BRACE JOVANOVICH, INC., for an excerpt from *No Man Is An Island* by Thomas Merton. Copyright © 1955 by The Abbey Of Our Lady Of Gethsemani; for an excerpt from *Smoke And Steel* by Carl Sandburg. Copyright © 1920 by Harcourt Brace Jovanovich, Inc., copyright © 1948 by Carl Sandburg.

HARPER & ROW, PUBLISHERS, INC., for an excerpt from *Pilgrim At Tinker Creek* by Annie Dillard. Copyright © 1974 by Annie Dillard; for an excerpt from *Little House On The Prairie* by Laura Ingalls Wilder. Copyright © 1935 as to text, by Laura Ingalls Wilder, copyright © renewed 1963 by Roger L. MacBride; for an excerpt from *Commentaries On Living* by J. Krishnamurti, edited by D. Rajagopal. Copyright © 1956 by Krishnamurti Writings, Inc.; for an excerpt from *What Is Man? And Other Essays* by Mark Twain. Copyright © 1917 by Mark Twain Company, copyright © renewed 1945 by Clara Clemens Samossoud; for an excerpt from *Charlotte's Web* by E. B. White. Copyright © 1952 by E. B. White.

HOLT, RINEHART AND WINSTON, PUBLISHERS, for "The Freedom Of The Moon" by Robert Frost from *The Poetry Of Robert Frost* edited by Edward Connery Lathem. Copyright © 1928, by Holt, Rinehart and Winston, copyright © 1969 by Holt, Rinehart and Winston, copyright © 1956 by Robert Frost.

Edited by Patricia LaFortune Dreier
Designed by Mansfield Drowne
Illustrated by Donna Perry
Type set in Trump Medieval